Level
2

The Nature Kid's Guide to
GECKOS

DAVID ANDERSON

LP Media Inc. Publishing
Text copyright © 2026 by LP Media Inc.
All rights reserved.

For information address LP Media Inc. Publishing,
30012 Variolite St NW, Princeton MN 55371
www.lpmedia.org

Publication Data

Geckos
The Nature Kid's Guide to Geckos — First edition.

Summary: "Learn all about Geckos, the Nature Kid Way"
— Provided by publisher.

ISBN: 979-8-89818-172-7

[1. Geckos – Non-Fiction] I. Title.

Title: The Nature Kid's Guide to Geckos

CONTENTS

GECKO GETAWAYS

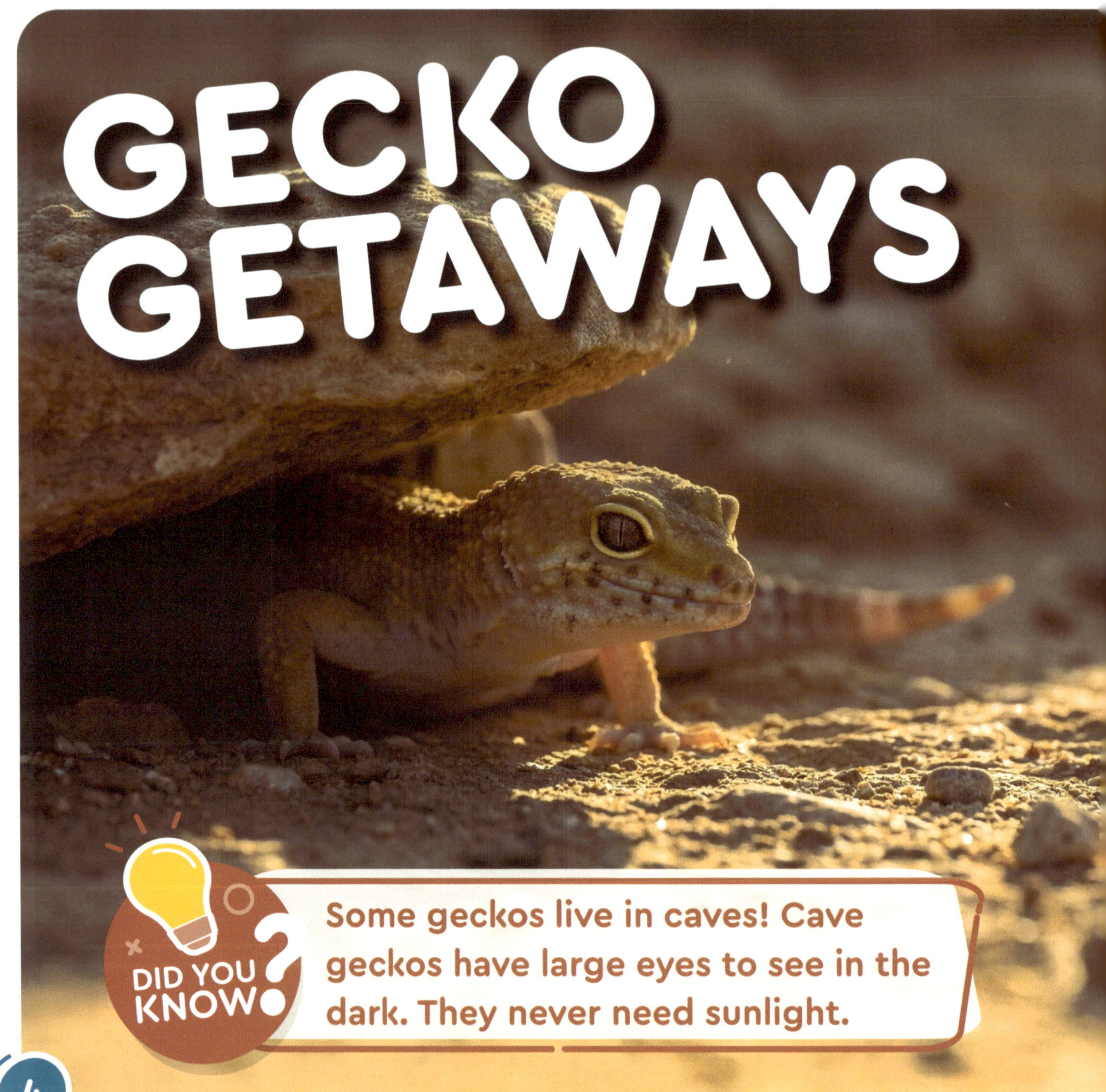

Some geckos live in caves! Cave geckos have large eyes to see in the dark. They never need sunlight.

Rustle! A leopard gecko crawls under a warm rock. It finds a cool spot.

Geckos live in many different places. Some need hot, dry land. Others need wet, steamy air. Each type of gecko has a home that fits its body.

Leopard geckos live in rocky deserts with sandy, dry ground. Days are very hot, but nights get cool. These geckos hide under rocks to stay safe from the heat.

Crested geckos need tropical forests. The air is warm and damp, and rain falls often. Tokay geckos like wet, warm places too. They climb trees in steamy rainforests.

GLOBAL GECKOS

Click! A house gecko climbs a wall. It is hunting for bugs!

Geckos live on every continent but Antarctica.

They live in Europe, Africa, and Asia. People brought them to America too. They rode here on ships long ago.

Mediterranean house geckos live near the Mediterranean Sea. Crested geckos live in New Caledonia. This small island is near Australia.

Tokay geckos live in Southeast Asia.

New Zealand geckos live in cold snowy mountains. They can live in snow!

BIG AND SMALL

Chirp! A tokay gecko calls from a tree. It grips the bark with sticky toes.

Geckos come in many sizes. Most are very small. They can fit in the palm of your hand!

Tokay geckos are some of the biggest. They grow up to 14 inches long. That is about as long as a ruler.

Day geckos are much smaller. Most are only 4 to 5 inches long. But the smallest geckos are tiny. They weigh less than a penny!

FUN FACT!

The Jaragua dwarf gecko can fit on a dime. It is one of the smallest reptiles on Earth.

9

STICKY
STUFF

Thump! A leaf-tailed gecko lands on a branch. It grips with sticky toes.

Geckos have amazing body parts. Their toes are covered with tiny hairs. These hairs are so small you cannot see them. They help geckos stick to walls and ceilings!

Leaf-tailed geckos have flat tails. Their tails look just like dead leaves. This helps them hide from enemies. Day geckos have bright green skin. Their colors help them blend into leaves.

Geckos also have unusual eyes. Most have no eyelids. They lick their eyes to keep them clean!

A gecko's toe hairs split into hundreds of tinier tips at the end!

SUPER
SENSES

Swoosh! A day gecko turns its head to watch a fly.

Geckos have super senses. Their big round eyes work like night vision goggles. When it gets dark, everything looks gray to us. But geckos still see the world in full color.

Geckos hear through small holes near their heads. Those holes are their ears!

They can even feel vibrations through their skin. If a bug lands nearby, a gecko knows it before it even looks.

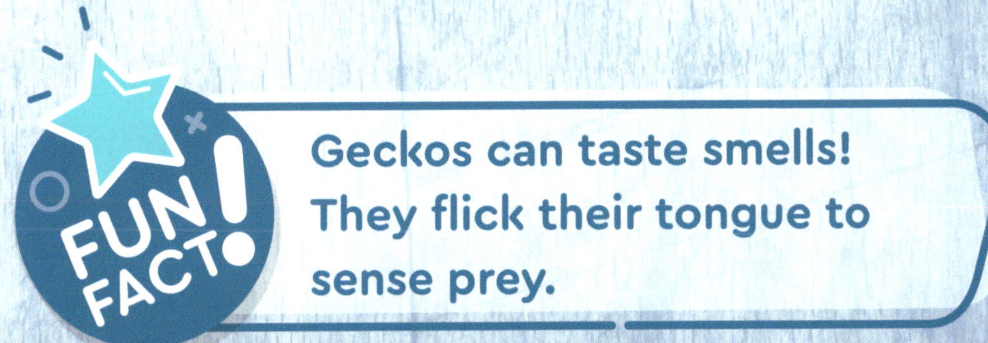

TRICKY TAILS

Most geckos can grow a new tail in about a month. But crested geckos cannot! If a crested gecko drops its tail, it is gone forever.

14

Snap! A snake grabs a gecko's tail. But the gecko runs away, without the tail!

Geckos have clever ways to stay safe. If a predator catches them by the tail, it falls right off! The tail flops and wiggles on the ground and distracts the predator while the gecko gets away.

Geckos are also masters of disguise. Leaf-tailed geckos look exactly like dead leaves, right down to the veins and brown edges.

Gargoyle geckos have bumpy heads that look just like rough stones.

Flying geckos press flat against tree bark and almost disappear. A predator could walk right past and never know a gecko was there.

DINNER
TIME

Munch! A crested gecko eats a ripe piece of fruit.

Geckos eat many kinds of food. Most geckos love to eat bugs. They munch on crickets, moths, and beetles. Some eat spiders too!

Crested geckos eat both bugs and fruit. They love to lick sweet **nectar** from flowers.

Mediterranean house geckos gather near lights at night. The lights attract tasty moths and flies. A hungry gecko can eat 16 bugs in one night!

Some geckos eat their own shed skin for nutrients!

SNAP ATTACK

FUN FACT!
Geckos only eat insects that are smaller than the width of their own heads to avoid choking!

Snap! A tokay gecko catches a bug in its powerful jaws. Yum!

Geckos are sneaky hunters. They stay very still and wait. When a bug comes close, they strike fast!

Tokay geckos hunt at night. They hide on walls and tree branches. Their big eyes spot bugs in the dark. Then they lunge forward and snap!

Leopard geckos hunt differently. They walk slowly across the ground. They stalk their prey like tiny cats. When close enough, they pounce! Their sticky tongues help them grab slippery bugs.

WATCH OUT

Screech! A Kuhl's Flying gecko jumps away as an Owl swoops by.

Many animals hunt geckos. Snakes are common predators. They find geckos hiding in trees and rocks. Some snakes eat geckos whole!

Birds also hunt geckos. Owls catch them at night. Hawks grab them during the day.

Large spiders catch small geckos in their webs. Near homes, cats and rats hunt geckos too. With so many hunters around, geckos must always stay alert!

Geckos will sometimes scream when scared! The loud noise startles attackers.

22

Shuffle! A leaf-tailed gecko hides against tree bark.

Geckos have clever ways to escape danger. But hiding is their best defense. Leaf-tailed geckos stay perfectly still. Their flat bodies blend into tree bark. Predators walk right past them!

Many geckos can run up to 7 miles per hour. This speed helps them zip into tiny cracks if a predator comes close.

Tokay geckos fight back. They will bite hard if grabbed.

Some geckos tear off their own scales to escape predators! Don't worry, the scales grow back.

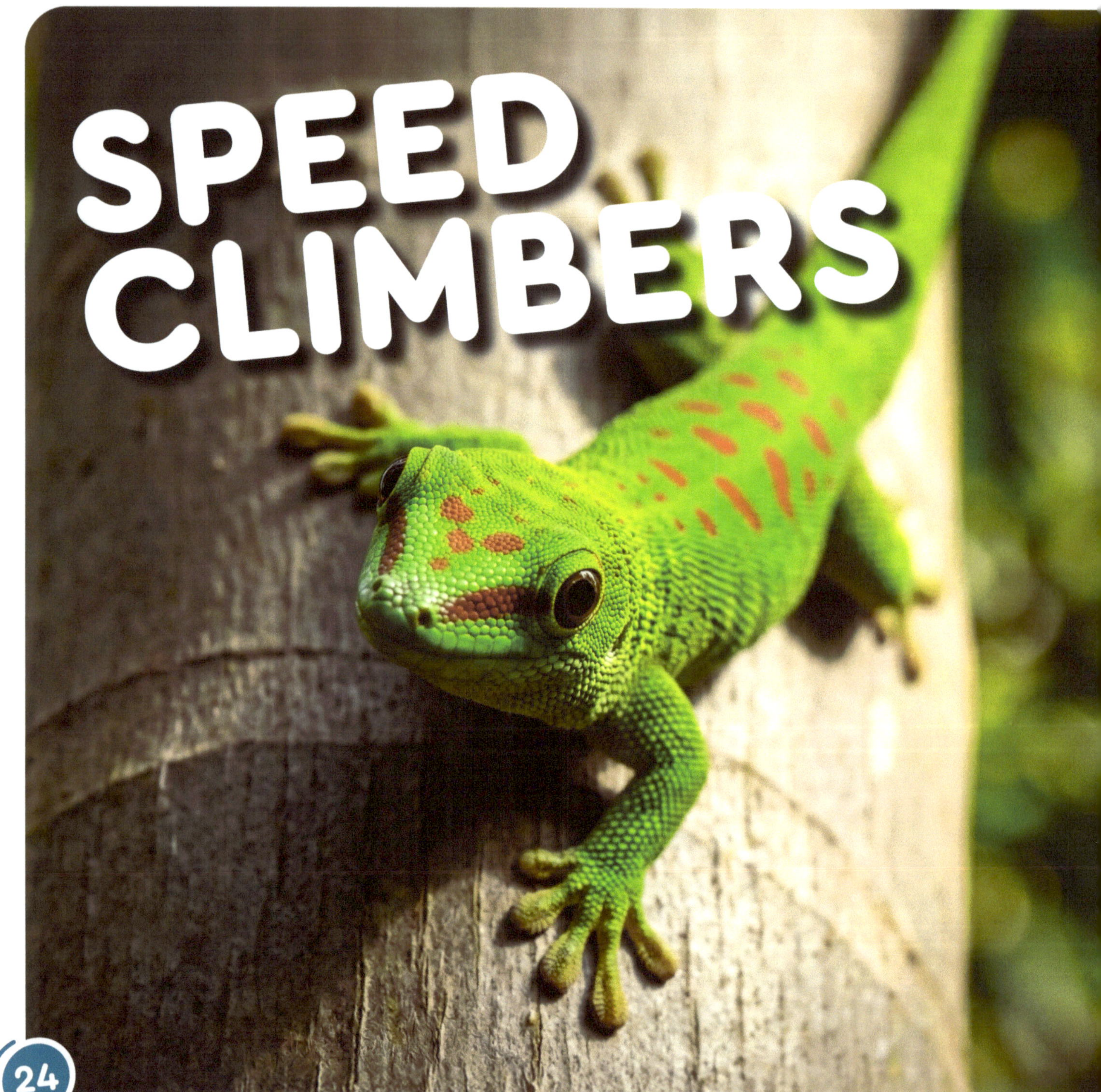

SPEED
CLIMBERS

Race! A bright green day gecko climbs straight down a palm tree!

Geckos are amazing movers. Most geckos can run up walls. They can even walk upside down on ceilings!

Flying geckos have special skin flaps. They spread these flaps wide and glide between trees.

Day geckos race along branches to catch bugs. Leaf-tailed geckos are different. They move slowly to stay hidden.

The flat-tailed house gecko can sprint across water! They slap the surface with all four feet so fast they barely sink.

DAY AND NIGHT

Now the day gecko calls out in the morning sun. He's ready to eat!

Most geckos are **nocturnal**. They sleep during the day and wake up at night. But day geckos are different. They love sunshine!

Day geckos hunt for food when the sun is out. Their bright green color helps them hide in sunny leaves.

Flying geckos are the opposite. These nocturnal geckos sleep all day. When darkness comes, they glide through the forest looking for bugs.

Some geckos change color between day and night. They turn darker at night, which helps them absorb more heat!

LONER LIZARDS

Some geckos use old scorpion burrows! This can be risky. They might meet a scorpion inside!

Rustle! A Mediterranean house gecko hides in leaves.

Most geckos live alone. They do not form groups or families. Each gecko finds its own spot to hide and hunt.

A gecko may pick a crack in a wall, a hole in a tree, or a space under bark. That spot becomes home.

Geckos do not have leaders. They do not follow other geckos. When two geckos meet, they often fight.

Males bite and wrestle over **territory**. They bark and chirp loudly to warn others to stay away. If a stranger gets too close, a gecko will puff up its body to look bigger.

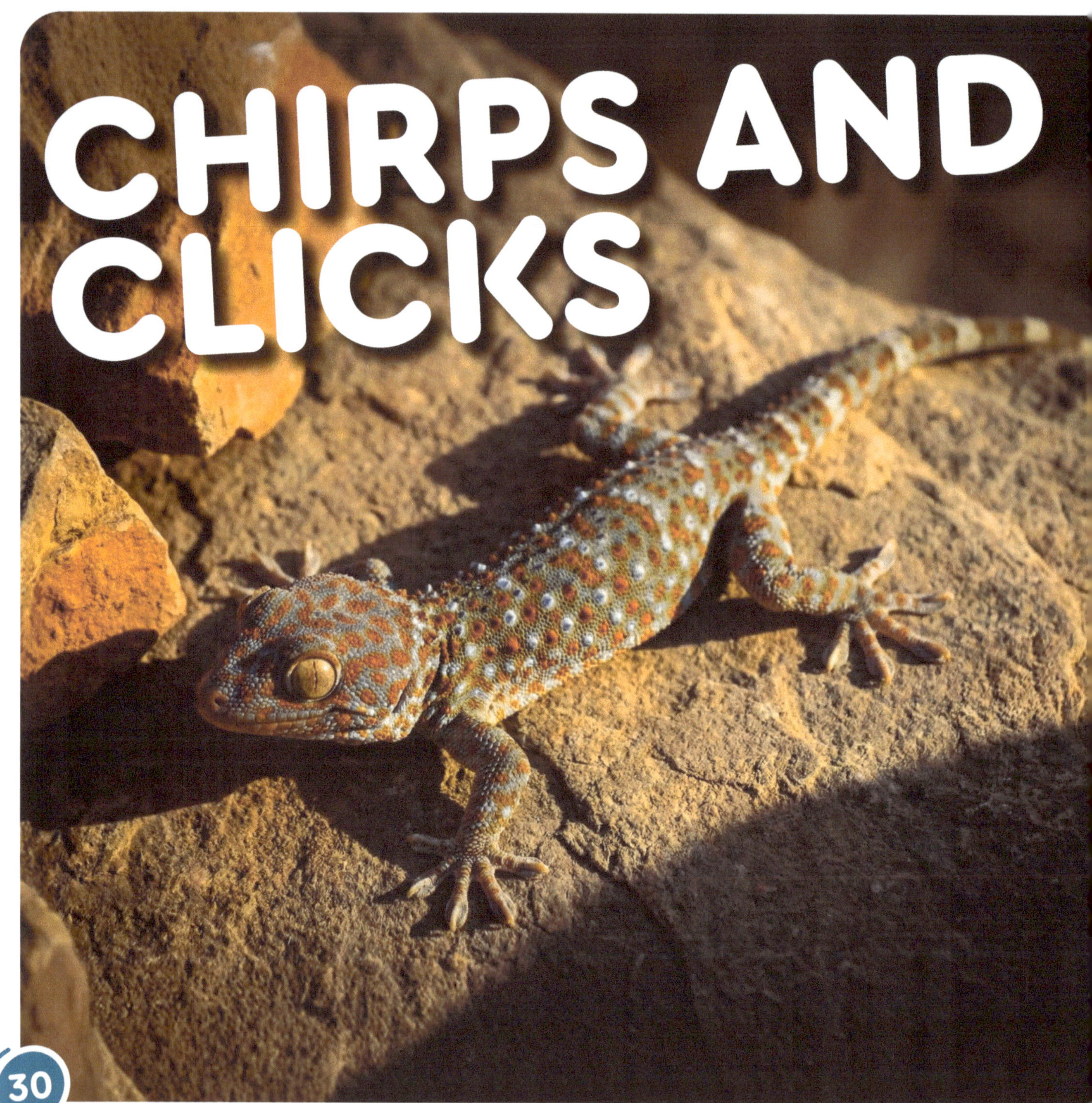

CHIRPS AND CLICKS
30

To-kay! A tokay gecko sits on a warm rock to soak up the sun.

Geckos make sounds. Most lizards are silent, but not geckos! Male tokay geckos are very loud. They call "to-kay, to-kay" again and again to warn other males to stay away and to attract a mate.

Mediterranean house geckos make soft clicks. Males chirp near walls at night to claim their territory. Each kind of gecko has its own sound. Female geckos listen for the loudest, strongest calls and choose those males as mates.

Tokay geckos have special calls. They can tell each gecko apart by its call!

TEENY HATCHLINGS
DID YOU KNOW?
Gecko eggs grow slower in cool weather. Some eggs can pause growing. They wait until the weather is just right!

Crack! A tiny crested gecko pushes out of its egg.

Baby geckos are called **hatchlings**. They break out of small, soft eggs. Some gecko eggs are the size of a jellybean!

Most geckos lay just one or two eggs at a time and hide them in a safe, dark place. Then mom leaves.

When the babies hatch, they are completely on their own.

Hatchlings look like tiny copies of their parents. They already have all their toes and spots. A baby leopard gecko is only 3 to 4 inches long. That is shorter than your finger!

MIGHTY MOMS

Thud! A tokay gecko guards her clutch of eggs.

Most mother geckos lay their eggs and leave. But Tokay geckos are different. Tokay mothers stay with their eggs and guard them for months.

They chase away bugs, lizards, and anything else that comes too close.

After they hatch, the mom leaves. Babies eat the leftover egg yolk for their first meal. They also eat their own shed skin, which is full of nutrients.

Within a few days, they must hunt for tiny bugs on their own.

Some gecko eggs hatch into boys or girls depending on temperature! Warm = males. Cool = females.

BORN
SURVIVORS

Chirr! A crested gecko plays on a mossy branch. Its big eyes look for bugs.

Geckos have lived on Earth for over 100 million years. They lived when dinosaurs did! The dinosaurs disappeared, but geckos kept going. They survived ice ages, floods, and fires. Today more than 2,000 **species** live all over the world, from jungles to deserts to people's houses.

Crested geckos were once thought to be gone forever. Scientists found them again in 1994. Now many people keep them as pets.

Geckos store fat in their tails. They can live for months without food by using that fat.

GECKO GAZING

Shuffle! A gargoyle gecko grooms its bumpy skin with its tongue.

Geckos live all around us! The best way to watch them is to stay quiet and move slowly. Geckos will run if you get too close.

Some geckos are easier to find than others. Day geckos are easy to spot on sunny walls. Gargoyle geckos are trickier since they hide in leafy plants.

Bring a flashlight for night watching. Enjoy from a few feet away!

Geckos can see 350 times better than humans in dim light! Their big eyes gather more light.

GLOSSARY

nocturnal
Animals that sleep during the day and are awake at night.

territory
An area that an animal claims as its own and defends from others.

species
A group of animals that look alike and can have babies together.

hatchlings
Baby animals that have just come out of their eggs.

nectar
A sweet liquid found inside flowers that some animals drink for food.